M

SALES MADE SIMPLE

A 4-step method for selling
anything to anyone that
always gets results.

JULIAN MARTIN

Published by
Media 21 Publishing Pty Ltd
(ABN 82 090 635 073)

30 Bay Street, Double Bay, NSW 2028
TEL (02) 9362 1800 FAX (02) 9362 9500
EMAIL m21@media21.com.au
WEBSITE www.media21publishing.com

© Julian Martin 2007
© Media 21 Publishing Pty Ltd 2007

National Library of Australia Cataloguing-in-Publication entry
Martin, Julian.
SMS : sales made simple.

1st ed.
ISBN 9781876624101 (pbk.).

1. Selling. 2. Sales personnel. 3. Success in business.
I. Title. II. Title : Sales made simple.

658.81

EDITOR/DESIGNER Charlotte Fish
PRINTED BY McPherson's Printing Group
SALES Stephen Balme EMAIL stephen@media21.com.au

Contents.

Introduction.

4 steps to successful sales.

$

The science of sales.

The great French impressionist, Renoir, was once asked what made him such a masterful painter. His simple answer was: *The six years I spent at art school learning how to draw lines.*

Yet when you look at his artwork, the last thing you actually notice are his lines; it's his use of colour and light that really strike you.

Like all talented people, Renoir understood that a knowledge of the basics was central to supporting his creative ambition. He strived to master the science of his craft which, in turn, became the foundation for his unique artistic expression.

In the same way, selling is very much a science as well as an art. It's a science because you have to follow some practical and systematic guidelines to make it happen.

It's an art because it requires expression, creativity and vision to practise it well.

The premise of this book is that if you understand and apply the science of selling correctly, the artist in you will flourish and you will become more natural and effective in the way you sell.

———

Over the last 20 years, my various sales teams and I have collectively generated over 100 million dollars' worth of sales.

We were successful for many reasons but, in retrospect, our high sales figures can clearly be attributed to just one thing. And like Renoir, when we applied this key factor we became devastatingly expert at reaching our objective – sales!

It's a simple approach to selling that equipped us to smash targets, poach deals from our main competitors, turn failed negotiations around and completely reinvigorate unmotivated sales teams that had lost their way.

I have had burnt out old sales executives literally run at me to celebrate their deals in childlike excitement after using this approach for the first time.

This same strategy has been instrumental in helping me climb the corporate ladder and win high-level senior sales positions. In fact, every time I talk to business people about it they tell me it's what they need to apply to their business.

Although simple, this formula is a highly effective sales method. It was developed by analysing the best sales practices and structures around today and breaking them down into four basic steps.

These four steps combine to create an intuitive structure that any sales professional can use to dramatically improve their results.

In addition, it is so easy to learn that it's also the perfect training platform for people just starting out, or for those with a more general interest in selling.

Most importantly, this method's logical steps guide you through the sales cycle in a way that ensures the buyer's needs have been fully understood and suitably met.

It is geared to significantly improve the customer's experience while positioning you to successfully close the sale.

Like an artist first learning to draw lines, when salespeople adopt this method they create a solid foundation on which to build their sales success.

————

The genius of this four-step method lies in its simplicity; its value in its effectiveness.

In many ways it represents the ABC of sales – that's why it's called Sales Made Simple (SMS).

Sales made simple.

The Sales Made Simple or SMS method is based on four progressive steps:

1 Asking open-ended questions in order to ascertain the customer's requirements.

2 Matching those requirements with the appropriate product or service.

3 Asking closed-ended questions to confirm that the customer's requirements have been met in order to close the sale.

4 Affirming the customer's purchasing decision.

Some simple interaction between these steps can occur if you need to work through any objections, but the straightforward nature of the above framework makes it easy to turn said objections around.

It looks simple, doesn't it?

As this book explores these four progressive steps in more detail, you will see how they become the 'lines' on which you can overlay your product knowledge and personality to become an expert and effective salesperson.

Step 1: Asking open-ended questions.

?

Open-ended questions help you to discover the customer's requirements.

An open-ended question is one that *cannot* be answered with a 'yes' or 'no'. These are the *how, what, when, why* and *who* questions.

As you think carefully about what sort of open-ended questions work well regarding your particular product or service, you will see how they form a crucial reference point within the negotiation. Your customer's key requirements will need to be satisfied in order to close the deal, so knowing them up-front gives you a significant advantage.

Step 2: Matching the need.

Once you are confident that you have asked the right questions and understand what the customer is looking for, you will be in a perfect position to demonstrate how your product or service meets those requirements.

These first two steps represent a classic 'needs resolution' approach to selling.

Step 3: Asking closed-ended questions.

≡ ?

Once you have matched the customer's requirements with a suitable offering, you are in a position to start closing.

A 'close' is a closed-ended question. It is contrary to an open-ended question in that it can *only* be answered with a 'yes' or 'no'.

For example:
Is this what you are looking for?
Is this in your price range?
Will you need this today?

In a simple sales situation, sometimes only one closed-ended question is needed to close the sale, however in most circumstances a number of closes are required to properly clinch the deal.

A series of closes is called a 'closing staircase'.

In the customer's mind, closes confirm that their requirements have been met and help them to feel satisfied. They also help to uncover any objections that might be hindering the sale from moving to its natural conclusion.

It is during Step Three that all negotiations are settled with closed-ended questions. The difference between discounting and negotiating is that when you discount, you drop your price or make concessions without any agreement for something in return; however when you negotiate, you adjust your price or position in return for something from the customer.

For example, in a situation where the customer is trying to bring the price down, in a negotiation you would close against the reduction. A typical question would be:

If I lower the price to the figure you're suggesting, would you commit to buying today?

All negotiations are known as 'conditional' closes; that is, if you say yes to *this*, I will do *that*.

———

Step Three is also where objections can arise but the SMS method deals effectively with these by simply returning to the first three steps:

1 Explore the specific problem thoroughly via open-ended questions.

2 Resolve or satisfy the problem.

3 Confirm that the problem has been resolved.

Steps One, Two and Three are cyclical in that if a problem or objection arises in the closing staircase, it's dealt with simply by running through the steps again with that one issue in mind.

Step Three (p. 88) explains in detail how you can *turn an objection into an opportunity* to close the deal.

In sales, a lot of mystery surrounds closing, but by knowing what form your closed-ended questions will take, and how and when to use them, you will be able to move a sale forward quickly and effectively.

Step 4: Affirming the sale.

≡ $

Once the sale has been closed, your next step is to affirm it.

This has to be the most underestimated and neglected sales step in the marketplace today.

This isn't just thanking the customer for their business. It goes further than that by complimenting the customer for making a good decision in relation to their original requirements.

Affirming the sale does three key things:

1 It helps deal with buyer's remorse and reduces the chance of a return. The customer will remember your affirmation if confidence in their decision starts to wane.

2 It deals with stress. It leaves both you and the customer feeling good about what's just happened. This is especially

helpful if the situation has become slightly awkward or uncomfortable after what may have been a big decision for the customer.

3 It leaves you and your customer with a final interaction that is a positive experience. You want to make it easy for the customer to come back, buy again, and refer you to others.

It's also simply polite!

Four steps that cover everything.

Don't underestimate the effectiveness of the SMS method.

Even if you use just one of the steps, it's going to improve the way you do business. Get all four steps down pat and you will revolutionise your selling ability.

Your confidence will grow in the knowledge that you recognise exactly where you are and where you want to go in *any* negotiation, rather than struggling to reach an agreement on a wing and a prayer.

Most importantly, your customers will be getting better service. The SMS method enables you to really understand their needs and, as a result, you will be confident that you are helping them to make a wise purchasing decision.

Other efficiencies will also develop. Deals will be closed more quickly and you will be qualifying prospects earlier and sorting out the timewasters before they have wasted your time.

Once you really understand and are comfortable with these four stages, you will be amazed by how easily you can shift in and out of them at will. You will never look back once you've experienced firsthand how effective they are.

It's your job to work out how to best adapt the SMS method to suit your particular product or service – the workbook sections in this book can help you with this. Indeed, this simple technique is so flexible that you can also experiment with it by including some of your own ideas. Then, if they don't work, you can easily fall back on the basic steps.

Remember that what is on offer here is the *science* of sales. Your own artistry and style will emerge as you develop a better understanding of this science.

Method or madness?

Method acting is another great analogy for the SMS approach. Method acting is one of the most popular acting techniques in the world and has been taken up, to some degree, by all of the greats: James Dean, Al Pacino, Richard Burton and John Travolta to name a few.

Like salespeople, even the most talented actors sometimes find it hard to deliver a top performance on demand, day after day.

So when the talent dries up, these professional artists fall back on their 'Method' to get them through.

The Method helps actors to draw upon real-life experiences and then project the associated feelings through the character they're playing. That's what made people like James Dean – who took Method acting to the limit – always look so credible and authentic.

The SMS method is similar in its ability to guide you through any sales situation, whether you are talented or unmotivated, on a good day or bad. It will allow you to develop a more genuine style of communication while drawing deals to their natural conclusion – all without your having to think too much about what you are doing.

A simple approach.

One of my passions is to see people succeed in business. Another is to see people's personalities come to the fore when they are selling.

The reason I love the SMS method is that its strategic framework supports you, while its simplicity makes it easy to wrap your own personality and product knowledge around it.

It is intuitive enough to not overshadow your unique and natural selling style, yet designed to drive the negotiation all the way home by the most direct path.

My sales career began in my early 30s, selling advertising space for a regional newspaper. Within a couple of years I was promoted to manage the paper's small sales team of five.

Although I had the gift of the gab, this first promotion challenged me to grow beyond my own 'art' of selling as I discovered that my sales instincts, however effective, were difficult to pass on to others. I began a passionate search to discover a more scientific approach to selling and this is when I started to think about a selling 'method'.

After five or six years of managing the newspaper's sales team and following some substantial growth in the business, I yearned for greater things. It wasn't long before I found myself in a fast-paced, highly competitive capital city working for blue-chip corporations and multi-billion dollar multinationals.

The sales targets became daunting and were often in the many tens of millions of dollars – most of my deals were now worth more than the regional newspaper's monthly turnover.

I experienced a colossal stretch in my confidence, despite a constant battle with feelings of inadequacy in this highbrow corporate world. I had no real qualifications at all – just my method, some basic sales instincts and sales record – while the people around me all had marketing or business degrees and spoke with an unfamiliar corporate jargon.

Nevertheless, I surprised myself by achieving greater levels of sales success than my highly qualified colleagues.

I attributed this to the fact that I had cut my teeth selling advertising space for that local newspaper – usually to small, savvy and often cash-strapped business owners who demanded a return on every cent they spent.

That environment had required tenacity and nerve as well as a high level of natural salesmanship and these were the qualities that gave me an edge I could not have learned at university.

———

Over the years I have sat in on hundreds of sales-training sessions and sales conferences. Being as passionate as I am about selling, I wholeheartedly absorbed everything on offer at these events and have seen almost every 'you beaut' sales-training model in existence.

What has always struck me as odd about the majority of sales-training models is how complex they are, because that complexity always seems to lead to a low take-up rate of what's on offer – the information simply doesn't sink in. Another problem with a lot of sales-training models is that they focus wholly on interpersonal behaviour without exploring much else.

It's as though they require the salesperson to wear a mask in order to win business – something that is hard to do and easy to spot. Never let a sales technique dominate your personality or authenticity. You know what I mean – nobody wants to deal with a technique. We would all rather experience genuineness of character.

Good salespeople can get all fired up and motivated by a day in the training room. However, because of the often complex and superficial nature of what's on offer, when it comes to putting the given techniques into practice they usually fall forgotten by the wayside.

This has always worried me because these kinds of sessions aren't cheap and you often find big companies spending a lot of money on sales training with little return.

That's why I always favoured a simple, focused approach and went on to develop the SMS method – which I can easily teach in a short session or on the job. It seems everything I've experienced in my sales career has led me to develop and refine this method, and the more I compare it with other (more complex) sales-training processes, the more I realise and appreciate its true value.

———

This book will present real examples of the SMS method's success, including a situation where the technique was followed, step by step, to turn around an $80 000 deal that had been declared dead and buried, and another where a deal worth four times that amount was poached from a competitor.

Sales managers, entrepreneurs and small business owners have a lot to gain from employing this method because, once their sales force start practising it, they can be confident that their team will be really listening to their customers and exploring every sales opportunity.

There is certainly something about having everyone sing from the same songsheet. It streamlines efficiencies, makes reporting easier and helps to develop a healthy and happy work environment. You quickly notice when someone is out of sync.

Another point worth mentioning here is that sales professionals are at high risk of burnout because of the emotional strain of continually trying to persuade people to buy. Add to this the pressure of meeting sales targets and dealing with disappointed or demanding customers and emotions can very quickly start to fray.

Stress and selling don't mix. The SMS method eliminates stress because it moves you away from relying on the power of persuasion and into the more natural realm of needs resolution. In fact, there is nothing persuasive about it.

It is just the simple process of asking the right kinds of questions at the right time and really listening to the answers.

What this book is not.

This book is not a manual on how to persuade someone to buy something they don't need or want – it is not a book on manipulation.

The SMS method simply doesn't work like that; it actually demands certain values and a level of transparency.

Essentially, it takes a brave approach to selling openly which is both sustainable and pure.

Indeed, you will find that the murkier things get ethically, the more you'll have to distance yourself from the method. Like most pure systems, it just doesn't work well in dodgy situations.

What this book is.

This book describes the SMS method – a selling technique you can always rely on – while exploring the fundamental tools you need to best describe, demonstrate and pitch your offering.

This effective sales method is comprised of four basic steps:

1 **Determining the buyer's requirements.**
2 **Matching those requirements.**
3 **Effectively closing (in relation to the requirements).**
4 **Affirming the sale.**

It's a map of the basics that anybody can learn and adapt to suit their own style, product or service.

It's a strong framework to guide you through any negotiation while simultaneously allowing your own personality to shine.

It's so simple and flexible that you can break the rules and experiment by working your own ideas into it. If they don't work for you, you can easily fall back on its basic steps.

It works equally well for developing marketing and advertising ideas.

It's the ABC of sales – designed to take the mystery out of selling.

It's a manual, a sales handbook and a workbook.

It's for everyone.

Step 1:

Affirming the sale.

Asking closed-ended
questions.

Matching the need.

**Asking open-ended
questions.**

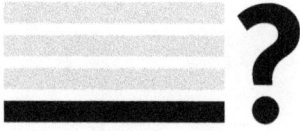

The open-ended question.

When selling, it's important to understand exactly what the customer is looking for before trying to sell them anything.

It seems obvious, doesn't it?

However, most people sell by making basic assumptions and then just pitching. The trouble is, when you don't fully understand what the customer's requirements are, you put yourself at great risk of sabotaging your pitch before you even get started. This applies equally to situations where you instigate the approach as to when the customer comes to you.

How you engage people in business is important.

Whether it's on the phone or face-to-face, niceties and politeness are crucial to success. However, this book doesn't go into the specifics of engagement strategies or techniques for answering the phone properly as some other sales training books do. These skills are a given, and hopefully you can work out what suits your particular culture or business environment.

So, the first SMS step focuses on what should be achieved at the start of any negotiation as it is fundamental to its success: an understanding of what the customer is looking for and why.

It's all about asking open-ended questions as they are the best way to discover the buyer's particular requirements. How and what you discover about your customer's needs early in the transaction will determine how successful you are in closing the deal.

Open-ended questions are questions that *cannot* be answered with a 'yes' or 'no'.

They are the *how*, *what*, *when*, *why* and *who* questions.

They are fantastic for investigating anything.

For example, compare these two questions:

Do you like to play football?
Why do you like to play football?

The second question is an open-ended question because it cannot be answered by a 'yes' or 'no', thereby revealing so much more than the first.

Here are some examples of simple open-ended questions that can be used for selling any product or service:

What exactly are you looking for?
What sort of experience have you had with this product (or service) before?
What brought you into my store?
Why do you like this one so much?
*What **aren't** you looking for?*
What are the absolute 'must-have' features you are looking for? And why?
Why are you looking for one of these?
Who will be using this?
What else have you seen on the market?
Which ones did you like and why?
How did you hear about us?
How often will you be using this service?
How soon do you need this repair done?
What do you need?
Where did you get your last one and why?
*What are the things you definitely **don't** want?*
What sort of budget did you have in mind for this?
What do you think about this one?

Again, these are all open-ended questions because they can't be answered simply with a 'yes' or 'no'.

Now consider what sort of open-ended questions would suit your product or service and make some notes at the end of this section.

Open- vs. closed-ended questions.

A closed-ended question is contrary to an open-ended question and can *only* be answered by 'yes' or 'no'.

A closed-ended question is also referred to as a 'close'.

Closed-ended questions are fantastic for confirming that the buyer's needs have been met, but are not appropriate for uncovering those needs in the first place.

Examples of closed-ended questions or 'closes' are:

Does this fit you comfortably?
Is this what you are looking for?
Would your wife like this one?
Is this within your budget?
Can you see anything in the store that you like?

Note the difference between an open-ended question and a close.

Of course, it is during closing that an objection can suddenly arise. Step Three (p. 88) covers this and explains how an objection to a close can actually be a very good opportunity.

Using closed-ended questions prematurely – especially at the discovery stage – can work against you and force the conversation into a dead end. That's why you should always start with open-ended questions.

Here's an everyday example of how open-ended questions might work in, for example, a lawnmower store.

Before showing the prospect anything, a good salesperson will ask a few basic, open-ended questions such as:

Could you describe the area that you are going to mow?
  What sort of surface area are we talking about?
What sort of machine was previously used for the job?
  How did that model work for you?
What special requirements do you have?
*What sort of features would you like your new lawnmower
  to have?*

These are all good open-ended questions which will help the buyer to explore and confirm – in their own mind – what they are looking for, while the answers they provide will help the salesperson to recommend an appropriate machine.

These questions get people thinking while helping to establish rapport and credibility.

In contrast, an unskilled salesperson might go straight in with closed-ended questions, hoping that the customer's reaction will steer them in the right direction. This trial-and-error approach typically begins with closed-ended questions such as:

Is this the sort of machine you're looking for?
Is there anything on the floor here that you like?
Out of these two machines, which one do you prefer?

This tactic corners the customer prematurely and results in their walling themselves off and struggling to regain control.

By using closed-ended questions too early in the transaction, the salesperson has also done nothing to help the customer understand what's on the market or what options are available to them.

Worst of all, the customer hasn't been given an opportunity to describe and explore what they are looking for. From this point, the salesperson will struggle to develop a dialogue with them.

Of these two approaches, it's obvious which one the customer would respond to best.

The salesperson that asks the customer open- rather than closed-ended questions *up front* will fully reveal and understand the customer's requirements, open up the conversation and establish a good connection.

This first SMS step is crucial to the eventual success of the deal.

+ These initial questions are far more important than just being smooth or polite. Used properly, open-ended questions are a tactic that will establish whether a sale exists at all and, if it does, how you can win it.

Hot buttons.

The one thing that your customer will be unlikely or unwilling to compromise on is their 'must-have' requirement or 'hot button'. It is *imperative* that you match and satisfy this major requirement, and with big-ticket items there are often more than one.

At this point, a good salesperson will listen very carefully and say as little as possible. The idea here is to prompt the customer to open up and disclose their requirements before you attempt to sell them anything.

Step One (asking open-ended questions) may seem a bit basic. However, it does take some insight to ask the right sort of questions to set up the rest of the sale.

Politely ask the right questions at the beginning of the conversation and listen very carefully. By uncovering and satisfying your customer's most essential requirements, you will position yourself to close the deal.

Of course, you will need to structure the questions in a way that compliments your product and not the competition's. It also takes some skill to refrain from trying to match and close until you get this first step right.

A good way to find a hot button is to start by asking your customer to name a few key requirements, and then ask which one of them is the most important.

When you uncover a genuine hot button or non-negotiable, must-have requirement that you know you can match, really run with it. Find out all about it and why it is so important to your customer. If you can, empathise and agree with them. Let the customer get passionate about it because if you're smart, you will enthusiastically refer to it in *every* step of your negotiation.

✚ With practice, your investigative ability will improve and you will really start to enjoy uncovering and establishing your customers' concerns.

This puts some of the care factor back into selling, making the whole process more enjoyable for both parties.

Using hot buttons.

Open-ended questions set you up for success because a buyer is often in research mode.

What better opportunity is there to establish credibility and make a connection with the customer as you explore their requirements with them? Then, when you're ready to move them on to Step Two and demonstrate just how you can meet those requirements, you will be in a position to offer qualified and relevant options that will influence the buyer's decision.

If you listen to an expert in any field, they do this quite naturally. It's the typical (good) lawnmower store scenario. The salesperson inquires about the job the customer is about to embark on and then offers some good advice and explains their best options.

With the lawnmower prospect for example, let's say it was established from the outset that ease of starting the machine was a big issue for them. So an electric starter motor would be an obvious 'must-have' or 'hot button' for the buyer.

When closing in this situation, a good salesperson would structure one of their closes like this:

Do you think that an electric starter motor like the one on this machine is something you need?

Yes, comes the obvious answer.

Are you ready for the next close?

*Well, its lightweight, has plenty of grunt to do the job on a lawn the size of yours **and** it has an electric starter motor.*
Do you like it?

What a great close. In fact, the deal is almost done – one more close would probably clinch it. Can you think of one? What about:

Is this mower within your budget?

Bingo! If the answer is yes, the deal is closed.

But what if the answer is no? What then? Step Three will explain how an objection can be used as an opportunity (depending on what is said) by taking the objection back to open-ended questions.

But in this case, the customer is clearly delighted and has said yes.

The next step is affirmation.

Loading the lawnmower into the customer's car, the salesperson says:

Well, I reckon mowing the lawn is going to take on a whole new meaning in your household, Mr. Jones. You're going to notice a huge difference with this machine – it's not just easier to use, it's so easy to start and a lot quieter than your old one. Your neighbours are going to appreciate that, and there's no doubt they'll be coveting this little beauty of yours!

Nice affirmation!
See Step Four (p. 112) for more on affirmation.

So, after such a wonderful customer experience, where do you think this customer will be telling his neighbours he bought his new lawnmower?

You've got it!

Using open-ended questions.

When I started in sales – selling advertising space for the local newspaper – I quickly discovered that asking open-ended questions was the most successful strategy.

When I asked my prospective customers how, why and where they had previously tried advertising, and with what results, they would open up willingly, hoping the conversation would lead to something positive.

It was obvious to them that I cared and genuinely wanted to establish what was best for them.

At the same time, this approach made it easy for me to find out what our main competitors were doing. They had been asking if the prospect wanted to advertise (a closed-ended question up front) and then trying to entice them with discount rates.

It was a fairly hollow offering that didn't impress.

On the other hand, I found what really worked was exploring the key objectives and what was, or wasn't, producing results. It's what's often referred to as a 'solution sell'.

It all seemed too easy as I began to win business by simply asking those more imaginative and thoughtful questions about the clients' products, their business, their budgets and their experience. A day or so later, I would be presenting them with an advertising campaign that best suited their need. We were constantly outselling the competition because we bothered to understand our clients' needs and demonstrated how they could be achieved through our paper.

Not only were we winning the business – often at rates 30–50% higher than our competitor – we were also winning customers' hearts because they could see that we genuinely cared. This method successfully resulted in some long-term advertising arrangements that were hard for our competitors to cannibalise, and our revenue grew from strength to strength.

———

To be honest, at that stage of my sales career I wasn't very strong at closing. I didn't really get it, and I thought it seemed a bit pushy. Even so, asking open-ended questions and matching the need were working really well.

When I began to understand what a close really was, and how to ask a series of them *naturally* in a closing staircase, my sales went into overdrive.

As a general rule, people who are good at open-ended investigation are usually not very good at closing and vice versa. It is important to get the balance right so that you can be confident with both.

Step Three (p. 88) examines closing in detail, and shows how returning to the customer's original requirements naturally lays the groundwork for the close.

Some useful open-ended questions.

Here are some examples of great open-ended questions:

When selling advertising space:
How do you currently advertise and how effective is it?
What services do you offer that are unique compared with your competitors?
What sort of promotions could you run alongside your advertising campaigns?
What time of year does your advertising achieve the best results?
What sort of returns would you expect from an advertising campaign?
What sort of budget do you have?

When selling a car:
What will you mainly use the car for?
Why did you respond to my advertisement?
What are the three most important things you look for in a car?
If you had to, what would you be prepared to compromise on?
*What **don't** you want in a car?*

When selling a service (e.g. cleaning):
What exactly are your needs here?
How would you like this job to be done?
What sorts of things do you expect from your cleaner?
How long do you think this job should take?
What was your last cleaner like – what did they do well, or not so well?
Can you describe your special requirements?

When selling your expertise (e.g. as a builder):
What are the most important qualities you look for in a builder?
What are your biggest fears regarding this job?
How would you like the quote to be structured?
How long do you expect this job to take?

Of course, these kinds of questions can be much more detailed – these examples are just guides.

––––

A really good open-ended question to ask in a proactive, cold-call situation is:

What is the best time for me to approach you with my product?

I have used this one a number of times to get my foot in the door. It usually results in a positive response that you can close the appointment on, such as:

The best time to catch me is in the morning. I could give you five minutes and if what you've got grabs me, I will give you more time.

Well, I can come out and see you early one morning, no problem. What day suits you? (Good open-ended question.)

Tuesday should be OK.

(Time to close the appointment.)
Shall I come by your office on Tuesday morning at 8am, then?

Yes, that would be a good time.

It's easy!

Successful selling is based on asking good open-ended questions at the beginning of the transaction.

The ultimate open-ended question.

An old boss of mine once taught me this valuable open-ended question:

If your budget wasn't an issue and you could have anything you wanted, what would it be?

I've never asked this question because I try to be more specific, but I do understand where my boss was coming from because the question essentially targets what all salespeople want to know – the customer's dream scenario.

In that particular business we were selling complex e-commerce solutions and business communications like corporate videos, up-market presentations, television commercials and websites.

It was a great job and we were targeting very large and successful corporations. I would often find myself presenting in boardrooms overlooking Sydney Harbour to very senior people like the CEO or the top executives of blue-chip companies.

Our presentation show reel was impressive, so I would begin the presentation with some knockout corporate video clip or animation to set the stage and gain some credibility.

Then, before I went on to present further, I would ask how they currently presented or positioned their company and what sort of aims they had in mind.

After a little investigation I would usually have some sort of insight into what they were planning for the future and could then tailor the rest of my presentation with that crucial information in mind.

It's such a simple and effective method, yet so many of my colleagues and competitors weren't operating like this.

They would generally launch into very complicated proposals and presentations which made them look clever but confused the client. In addition, they would rarely ask how the client did business or what their future plans were.

Often, the only research they had was gleaned from the client's website, without considering that the information might be outdated or only customer-focused.

Again, too many assumptions and *assumptions don't sell.*

Without having made a connection with the client, they would spend days putting together totally irrelevant proposals because they didn't really understand the client's immediate needs!

Meanwhile, I was sticking to my strategy. I would ask about the client's plans and requirements up front and then design my pitch to win the business.

I would listen patiently and take notes, often using their own words in my proposal to make it gel. I would explore their essential requirements with them before I put forward a proposal or began to pitch.

In that job, I was promoted from business development manager to sales director within three months.

The reason for my success wasn't because I was better than anyone else; it was because I was seen to stick to a basic formula. As a result, I appeared less stressed than my colleagues and won more business with less effort.

————

Open-ended questions are used up front to discover the customer's requirements and 'must-haves' or 'hot buttons'.

Open-ended questions *cannot* be answered with a 'yes' or 'no'. They are the *how, what, when, why* and *who* questions that genuinely reveal the customer's needs.

Where possible, avoid closed-ended questions early on.

The idea is to gain such a thorough understanding of the customer's needs that you will be able to match your product or service to it perfectly.

What sort of open-ended questions would work well for your product or service?

Keep in mind what you are trying to sell, the strengths of that product, and the type of people you are targeting.

Step 2:

Affirming the sale.

Asking closed-ended
questions.

Matching the need.

Asking open-ended
questions.

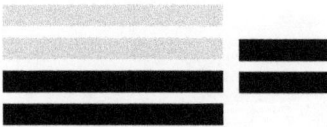

Matching and pitching.

After you have asked some appropriate open-ended questions and established the customer's requirements and/or 'hot buttons', the next step is to match them.

You now need to demonstrate, as effectively as possible, that your particular service or product satisfies those requirements.

This is sometimes referred to as 'needs resolution' – identifying a need and resolving it.

The style of your pitch can vary greatly in content and messaging depending on the situation.

Matching the need could take the form of a demonstration, a presentation, a test drive or a sample. Your offering could be presented via email or telephone, or in a proposal or formal quote. Perhaps it requires a face-to-face meeting – an informal chat in a café or a boardroom presentation. In fact, it could be a combination of any of the above, and more.

Although the form of your presentation will depend on many things, such as your market, customers, environment and budgets, remember that your pitch is something you can constantly improve over time.

––––

The second step of the SMS method is about developing the key messages that work for any product or service.

Like the first step, the same basic principles apply here – no matter what you are selling.

Step Two also explores three different ways of developing an appropriate match or pitch.

These are fairly traditional strategies and best practised in true sales environments, however they are by no means final.

There will be other ways that suit your particular business that no one has yet thought of, so keep your mind open to alternate possibilities.

The point to remember here is that it's at *this* stage of the sales cycle that you pitch your product – not until you fully understand your customer's needs and before you begin to close.

Developing a pitch.

Here are three ways to develop a pitch:

1 **Unique selling points.**
2 **Features, advantages and benefits.**
3 **Value propositions.**

You can use just one of these to formulate your pitch or pick and choose across the lot; it depends on how complex your market, product or service is. Incidentally, all three techniques work extremely well for developing marketing and advertising material.

However, these three suggestions are simply guidelines – feel free to utilise more imaginative or pertinent ideas, just make sure you stick to the task of matching the need.

Remember that what you are trying to do here is match the customer's requirements.

1. Unique selling points – USPs

This is probably the simplest way to approach matching your product to your customer's needs.

USPs are the qualities that set your particular product or service apart from the rest; they are the things that are uniquely yours.

They're not just standard features; they're the ones that make your product stand out as better or different.

USPs are similar to (and sometimes described as) your 'point of difference'.

Here are some examples of USPs:

– a money-back guarantee
– free delivery
– a unique manufacturing feature
– a special ingredient
– free training
– high quality parts
– handmade
– specially chosen
– environmentally friendly
– in excellent condition
– years of experience

Or it could simply be your passion and expertise.

What you should be looking for are the things that make your offering *special*.

Whatever your product or service, it's good to establish at least one USP for it.

Better still, have a number in mind so that you can select the right ones to suit differing customer requirements.

Can you name and describe two USPs in regard to your product or service?

2. Features, advantages, benefits – FABs

FABs are different to USPs because they comprise three specific aspects. FABs are effective because they force you to thoroughly consider your products or services.

It's best to have both of these up your sleeve – USPs for quick statements and FABs for more detailed conversations.

Features.

Features are the tangible operating systems, elements, processes or functions that make your product or service work.

Of course, these features are the ones that naturally meet the buyer's requirements.

For example, the offering could be lightweight, homemade, user-friendly, chemical-free or an example of the latest technology.

The best features are simple to explain and clearly suited to the customer's requirements or 'hot buttons'.

The features of a product could include:

– lockable casing
– all the latest gadgetry

- easy-open pop-top
- easy starter motor
- push-button release system
- leather seats
- 24-month money-back guarantee
- battery-operated
- easy access
- one size fits all
- double garage
- surround sound
- child safety
- certain specifications
- size, colour or ingredients
- 0-100 in 4.8 seconds

Depending on the product, the list is endless.

In a service industry, features could include:

- use of the highest quality products
- 24-hour service
- a helpline
- free pick-up and delivery
- years of experience
- the latest technology

What are the most impressive features of your product or service? How could you best describe them?

Advantages.

An advantage is an element that makes your product or service superior, or gives it a more favourable position in the transaction. It's the *edge* that it provides within a particular situation or during its use.

Typical advantages are:

– greater speed
– higher quality
– a brand you can trust
– a more economical option

An advantage can also be a less tangible (but equally valuable) factor such as your qualifications or experience, especially in regard to services.

In fact, your expertise could be the most valuable thing you have to offer. It may well be one of the 'hot buttons' your customer is looking for, especially when it comes to services like mechanical repairs, construction, architecture and dentistry, for example.

Advantages are usually powerful statements – *every* astute buyer wants to know what advantages their purchase will result in, and to feel that they have made the right decision.

The advantages you can offer are important to your customer, especially if they correspond to their essential requirements.

What advantages does your product or service offer?

Benefits.

A benefit is simply the way a product or service improves or promotes something for the customer.

From a buyer's point of view, a benefit results in their having more time, more room, more energy, or even more money.

It's what this product or service will do for the buyer and how it affects them.

Benefits of products could be:

– ease of assembly
– faster access
– greater reach
– longer lasting
– user-friendly

Benefits of services could be:

– fast results
– service with a smile
– quick turnaround
– *we will take care of this for you*
– *we save you time*

What short- and/or long-term benefits does your product
or service offer?

How will this product or service match or supersede your customer's requirements?

_____

_____

_____

_____

_____

_____

_____

_____

_____

_____

_____

_____

_____

_____

_____

_____

_____

_____

_____

_____

_____

_____

What kind of short-term benefits are you offering? Will the customer see an immediate improvement in their life?

Putting FABs into practice.

Keeping your FABs uppermost in your mind and stringing them together in a pitch is not as easy as using USPs but once you have practised it a few times, presenting your FABs will come to you more naturally.

> ✚ You will have a huge advantage over your competition if you promote your FABs clearly because they really show the customer how your offering meets their needs, not just in terms of its features but in what it means to them.

Here's an example of how FABs could work in the lawnmower store from Step One. In an effort to match the customer's requirements, a good salesperson might say something along these lines:

*This lawnmower is lightweight and has good safety features [**features**] which means you'll finish the whole job more quickly [**benefit**] and feel a lot safer when you're negotiating the slopes in your garden [**advantage**]. It also has an electric starter motor [**feature**] that makes starting easier [**advantage**].*

*These user-friendly features [**feature and benefit**] will leave you feeling far less tired when you've finished the job [**benefit**] and this will give you more time to do the other things you like doing in the garden [**advantage**].*

It is helpful to keep the competition in mind when you adopt this strategy. If you know your product is superior, use your FABs to explain why (without naming the competitor) and really emphasise the relevant points. Remember, every buyer is constantly evaluating and analysing in order to make the right purchasing decision, so tell them what they need to hear in order to swing their decision your way.

A good understanding and explanation of your product or service's features, advantages and benefits really puts your customer in the picture. With a little practice, your FABs will come to mind more readily and you will be able to select the right ones for each customer with ease.

Which features give your product or service an advantage over others in the market and how will these features benefit the buyer?

Try presenting a product or service using FABs.

What sort of open-ended questions (asked at the beginning of the sales cycle) would best position you to present your leading FABs?

Here are some good examples of FABs to use when selling real estate:

Features:
– the number of rooms
– the size of the garden
– security
– location

Advantages:
– safe for children
– close to work
– nothing to do, just move in

Benefits:
– a great investment
– suits your requirements perfectly
– your own home – no more renting

Here are some suitable FABs to use when selling a car:

Features:
– economy
– large boot
– easy to drive
– five doors
– fuel-efficient engine

Advantages:
– bigger than your current car

– will save you money on petrol

– golf clubs will fit in boot

Benefits:

– safe

– roomy

– low-maintenance

3. Value propositions – VPs

A 'value proposition' or VP is the value of your offer from the buyer's perspective – it's what matters to them.

To find a VP, put yourself in the buyer's position and try to understand what they are looking for and why. Your open-ended questions should give you the insight to accurately establish the VP for any customer.

In fact, there can be a number of basic VPs for certain products and services. For example, a VP for the lawnmower buyer was the machine's easy start – he can place a value on that. Another VP was the fact that it was lightweight and easy to manage. In combination these features make for a strong value proposition.

People are often dropping hints and clues for VPs in their answers to open-ended questions: *Oh yes, my wife is sick and tired of our old washing machine!*

And there's the value proposition: a happy wife.

Using USPs, FABs and VPs.

For a few years I was the corporate development director for an aid organisation. The organisation lent money to the needy while providing them with basic business training. The aim was to give these people a chance to work their way out of poverty.

Amazingly, 98% of the loans were repaid and this meant that the money could be *recycled* as new loans to other people – it's called micro-enterprise development.

It was my responsibility to raise large cash donations from blue-chip corporations, high net-worth individuals and churches for one-time donations of $10 000 to $450 000.

We also sought to engage with these organisations and corporations for volunteers and pro bono offerings like marketing expertise, accounting or legal services, software and the like.

Presenting the organisation's work was exciting because it was such a clever concept and most people hadn't heard of it before. However, it was also quite complex so we decided to develop two key value propositions.

The first value proposition was that the loan would be repaid and recycled out to another person in need.

To a major donor, that proposition held significant value. The fact that their donation was going to keep on working ad infinitum (even after their death) really appealed, especially to business people who understood the value of capital investment.

The second value proposition was that the loan was a hand 'up', not a handout.

Helping needy people to help themselves and escape poverty was viewed as highly worthwhile and valuable. It was not a short-term fix, bandaid solution or act of charity.

The loan recipient would receive extensive training to steadily develop the entrepreneurial talents that would lift them out of poverty and ensure they didn't return to it. The program focused on breaking the mindset associated with poverty while simultaneously working on a more practical level.

The value proposition here was that the donor was partnering with specific individuals to help them break free of poverty and they could also be sure that their money was working – in every sense of the word.

Once I had uncovered the donor's motivation through the use of open-ended questions, I would press home one of these value propositions (or both) before I would even consider closing on what they might want to give, and when.

The use of value propositions in these cases really helped the donor to appreciate how we understood and matched their own charitable motivations.

When presenting the organisation's FABs, I had a lot of material to work with. A significant **feature** was that the loan money was being lent at local bank rates which were 75% below the rates the local loan sharks were offering. The **advantage** here was that the recipient would actually be able to see results fairly quickly as they developed their small business.

I know this one is hard to believe, but the **benefit** of this was that the recipient didn't have to mortgage their children as labour to guarantee the survival of their loan. The local moneylenders would actually make their loan recipients *mortgage their children* if they couldn't repay the loan (at their exorbitant interest rates).

Another **feature** of the program was that it provided business training. Every week, the loan recipients would meet in groups to make their repayments and receive training for an hour. They also cross-guaranteed their loans which meant that they became accountable to each other.

This had a number of other **benefits**, the main one being that if someone in the group was having problems repaying the loan, the others would either support them or peer pressure would compel them to come up with the money. This was a major factor in establishing the organisation's high repayment rate.

These were great FABs which I consciously thought about and tailored to individual donors once I had established their requirements – in this case their motivation and reasons for wanting to help others.

Another **advantage** was that the recipients (we called them clients) were not getting a handout and therefore not becoming welfare-dependent. Yet another **advantage** was that the client's whole family was positively inspired, not just because of their increased earnings but because the entrepreneurial skills, business knowledge and sense of hope were all being passed on to the other family members by example.

The **benefits** were manifold but the primary ones were seeing these people break free of poverty combined with the positive changes in the local community as more commerce and trade developed in the area. There was also a **USP** – the organisation was unique in providing basic business training plus advice regarding health issues such as AIDS and domestic violence.

By consciously developing good FABs and VPs, we were in a position to really motivate the donors to give generously and with the confidence that their donation would have a remarkable impact.

Clearly, this example is rich with features, advantages and benefits but they are found (to varying degrees) in all products and services. You just have to uncover and develop them.

——

Remember how the 'good' salesperson in the lawnmower store scenario asked smart open-ended questions, establishing the customer's primary needs for a lightweight, easy-to-start, easily maintained machine. The salesperson then looked to the relevant FABs that matched the customer's need.

They discussed the electric start [**feature**] and how it would make the whole job less stressful [**advantage**] and finished in less time [**benefit**].

The salesperson may even look for a **USP** such as the fact that this particular model comes with a year's free service. In addition, a **VP** like reliability is appropriate here as the brand of mower is renowned for excellent engineering that would never let the buyer down.

How would you present your product or service using FABs?

Can you think of two VPs that your regular customers
might appreciate?

What USP initially comes to mind for your business?

_____

_____

_____

_____

_____

_____

_____

_____

_____

_____

_____

_____

_____

_____

_____

_____

_____

_____

_____

_____

_____

Case studies and testimonials.

Case studies and testimonials are great ways to demonstrate how your product or service works by utilising the value other customers have gained from it.

Testimonials.

A testimonial is a quote or statement that endorses your product – you can never have too many of them.

To obtain them, you will need to ask previous customers how things are going, and whether they are pleased with their recent purchase and why.

By the time the salesperson in the lawnmower store has closed the sale using the SMS method, they will be in the perfect position to ask the buyer if it would be OK to call him in a few weeks to see how things are going. The salesperson will then have an opportunity to draw out the testimonial at that time.

––––

When I bought my last car, I had one major issue with the brand I was considering.

To be honest, I loved the car but I was concerned about its reliability. The salesman then provided me with a terrific piece of feedback that a previous customer had given him after taking an outback trip. He said the only thing that had gone wrong was that one of the six speakers had cut out. That was enough to erase my concern and I bought the car. Incidentally, it's given me no trouble at all.

Testimonials are extremely useful. If you get some really good feedback on your product or service, it's worth asking your customer's permission to use it as a written testimonial to promote your product. Even better, put it on your website or in your marketing literature.

Some people are happy to endorse products and services but others aren't, so *make sure you get their consent* and be careful how you use their comments. A testimonial isn't necessarily an endorsement but it is a statement of satisfaction.

Case studies.

A case study is basically a more complex testimonial.

A case study thoroughly explores the customer's core issues, their requirements, how you worked together, how you helped to recognise and then solve their problems, and the overall outcomes.

Case studies are most appropriate for 'solution selling'. That's when you adapt a product (or product set or services) to meet a buyer's specific requirements in order to achieve a 'customised solution'.

The ideal case study would demonstrate how you worked with the customer to establish their 'brief'. It would then examine the solutions you produced and the way you delivered and integrated those solutions with the customer's concerns. Finally, the study would explore and summarise the results.

I have used in-depth case studies when selling intranets, websites and e-commerce solutions, especially to big corporations. The buyer needs to know how the briefing process works and what sort of timelines and milestones are established up front for signing off on various stages of the project. They want to be sure that someone else has had a positive experience with you. With business-to-business sales, the buyer's job can be on the line if they make a mistake or haven't applied due diligence in choosing the right supplier.

Salespeople use case studies to establish credibility, trust and confidence, especially with new customers.

––––

I have always focused on organising a number of happy customers as both referrals and case studies.

I usually set this up by taking a customer out to lunch two or three months after they have purchased from me. I start by asking them a lot of open-ended questions about the results they've achieved. If it's all very positive, I then ask if they mind my using their comments as a referral.

Nine times out of ten they are happy for me to do so.

After the lunch, I send the customer an email thanking them for their time and confirming that they have agreed to be used as a referral. I then write up the case study and forward it to them for approval. Again, nine times out of ten they approve it, and even go so far as to ask if they can use certain parts of it for their own marketing or sales purposes.

Of course, satisfied customers are a prerequisite for this to even be possible. But if you have used your SMS method properly you should have no trouble with this.

If an objection does arise during closing and you can see how a testimonial could clear it up, go back to your open-ended questions and clearly establish what the objection is about; that is, what customer requirement isn't being met. Then move to match the requirement with the testimonial and close it with a *Does that satisfy your concern?* type of question.

_____

I like to use testimonials because they tell the story of what my company or product is all about, as well as being the perfect way to match my customer's requirements.

Obviously, with smaller products and inexpensive items you don't necessarily need formal case studies or testimonials but, like the car salesman I bought from, a simple bit of honest feedback from another customer is always handy.

Build up a bank of testimonials or case studies to use during Step Two when matching your customer's needs.

Writing a proposal.

When writing letters or proposals, always be direct and don't use too many superlatives like *this **fantastic** product* or *our **extraordinary** money-back guarantee.*

People are busy and they want to be able to read things quickly and easily. They are looking for facts, not fluff. The best thing to do is get straight to the point.

I have seen 20-page proposals sent out for small jobs and you just know that there's no way anyone is going to read it all. The problem here is that if a prospect hasn't read your proposal thoroughly because it's too complex and longwinded, they will be nervous about signing off and it will be almost impossible to close the sale.

Follow this easy format for clear proposals:

1   Executive summary. Even though it opens your document, this is best written last. It outlines the contents of the proposal but doesn't mention cost.

2   Briefly describe the customer's business to show that you understand it.

3   Briefly outline your business.

4   Outline the basic objectives and requirements of the project that you are pitching for.

5   Outline your creative ideas, solutions and recommendations that meet the objectives and requirements.

6   Outline timelines and key milestones on how you would physically deliver the job.

7   Itemise costs, culminating in an overall cost or quote.

8   Outline your credentials, case studies and testimonials.

9   Terms and conditions can follow this, but I usually don't supply them until the proposal has been read. If I can close on the content of the proposal, then on the terms and conditions (as steps in a closing staircase), I am in a prime position to close the sale.

————

The best way to present your finished proposal to a customer is to read it with them.

Too many people spend hours writing their proposal and then just attach it to an email or letter, hoping that the prospect will open it immediately and push everything else aside to read it.

This is far too risky!

The best thing to do – having established that the client actually wants a written proposal – is to agree that when it's ready, you will take the time to go over it with them. Then, if there are any issues, they can be clarified quickly (and even closed on) and you can openly convey some of your passion and enthusiasm for what you're selling at the same time.

For some sales, especially smaller ones, you might pitch or quote via email or telephone, but remember that the best pitch happens when the customer's requirements are thoroughly understood. You should also confirm that they have fully grasped your proposal by asking a closed-ended question.

Once you've done that, you can get onto the closing staircase.

If you apply the first two SMS steps to any transaction, you will find yourself in the perfect position to close the deal.

Step 3:

Affirming the sale.

Asking closed-ended questions.

Matching the need.

Asking open-ended questions.

The closed-ended question.

It's time to start closing when you are confident that the first two steps have been properly completed; you have uncovered the customer's requirements and matched them with your product or service.

Closing is all about confirming that the customer's needs have been met and then steering the negotiation to reach its ultimate conclusion – a sale.

In sales, a 'close' refers to a closed-ended question.

A closed-ended question is contrary to an open-ended question in that it can *only* be answered with a 'yes' or a 'no'.

Here are some examples of closed-ended questions:

Do you like what you have seen here?
Does this fit your budget?
Is this the sort of quality you were looking for?
Do you think your wife would like this?
Do you like this colour?
Is this what you are looking for?
Is there anything you don't understand about this?
Would you like to buy this one?

Can you see how closed-ended questions can only be answered with a 'yes' or a 'no'?

These simple examples show how closed-ended questions not only confirm that the requirements have been met, but that each question also moves the negotiation in the direction of a sale.

Ideally, your close should reference the customer's primary requirements and 'hot buttons'.

For example, a car buyer is a keen golfer and in Step One you established that he needs a big boot for his golf clubs. In this situation, one of your closes should be:

Would your golf clubs fit comfortably into this boot?

Or perhaps a buyer is looking for special shoes for a wedding. An appropriate close would be:

Will these shoes go well with your outfit?

The closing staircase.

In a simple sales situation one closed-ended question can close a transaction, however in most circumstances a number of closes are needed to properly clinch the deal.

A *series of closes* is called a 'closing staircase'.

A closing staircase is where you line up a few strong closes in a row in order to position the negotiation for the final close to complete the deal.

Closing is rather like herding sheep. You use closes to herd the sheep (the requirements) into the sheep pen and close the gate (the sale).

Climbing the closing staircase.

Recently, I decided to buy a new electric shaver. I found a store that specialised in shavers, with a huge display that took up the whole wall.

The young salesman worked well to show me that one shaver in particular met my requirements. I told him it was a bit more expensive than I had expected, but that I was definitely considering it. While I was thinking this through, he suddenly tried to close:

Would you like me to get one of these from out the back for you?

He took me completely by surprise and although, as a sales trainer, I was pleased to see him trying to close the deal, it was far too early and it startled me.

The trouble was that it was his first and only close.

I felt cornered because I needed a bit more time to think and perhaps consider why I should buy that shaver. I just wasn't quite ready to buy, but he had left me with nowhere to move so I went cold and just said: *I'm not sure yet.* He had nowhere to go with me now, either. I felt awkward and wanted to leave the store as quickly as possible, which I did.

However, if he had taken me up a closing staircase, he may well have made the sale. He had a bit to work with too – there was a $50 cash-back offer that he had already told me about. He could have worked that into his closing staircase, which might have gone like this:

I understand that this is a little over your budget, but can you see how this model is far superior to the ones at your budget level and has much better features for you?

I definitely would have said 'yes' to that first close. Then he could have continued with another close:

Do you like it? Does it do what you want your new shaver to do?

He would have known he was on safe ground there as he could see that I liked it and he had already done a great job of showing me its FABs. So I would have provided him with another 'yes' and another step up his closing staircase. He could have come in with a third close here:

As you said, Sir, it's a bit over your budget but it does have the $50 cash-back deal with it. You have to agree that's a pretty good offer.

Yes, I would have to agree.

Here comes the fourth close:

It looks as though this shaver is the right one for you, Sir. Do you think it might be worth stretching your budget for?

Or perhaps:

Even though it's a bit over your budget, you would have to agree that it's very good value.

I would have agreed with both those points. Then he could have smiled confidently at me and made his final close:

Would you like me to get one from out the back for you, Sir?

And at that point, I know I would have said 'yes'.

Closing prematurely or without a number of preliminary closes can really work against you. This is why a closing staircase works so well.

Incidentally, I returned to the store a week later, bought that shaver from the salesman, and explained to him what had happened when he tried to close the sale too early.

I explained the principle of a closing staircase to him and he was grateful for the advice. He is now convinced of the benefits of using a closing staircase, which will impact positively and dramatically on his future sales career. In turn, I am grateful for such a good example to illustrate the closing staircase.

––––

Take progressive steps.

As a general rule, you should check that the buyer's needs have been met before you mention budget or price, and then move on to the final close, which is to ask for the order.

When I was selling with proposals or quotes I would always close around the simple things first, such as:

Do you understand the proposal?
Does it address the brief you gave me?
Is there anything in it you don't need or understand?
Have we addressed all your objectives?
Have we missed anything?
Do you have any feedback you want to give me?

I would then move forward to discussing how the price sits, whether or not everyone is on the same page and so on, and work through any objections before finally closing.

Objections and the closing staircase.

In a perfect world, all the closed-ended questions on your closing staircase would be answered positively and you would close the deal easily.

Unfortunately, in reality this doesn't always happen and it's at this stage that you may be confronted by objections.

Fortunately, the structure of the SMS method ensures that you know that this is where objections can possibly arise and that you can handle them systematically from this point while remaining in the closing staircase.

Earlier, I used the analogy of herding sheep. Like a shepherd, you sometimes have to be thoughtful and strategic in how you round up all the requirements. Occasionally, one will run away from the herd and you need to keep the others grouped together as you chase after the runaway. That 'runaway' would be something like an objection, and you need to hold all the requirements (that *have* been met) together on the closing staircase while you bring the objection back into line.

An objection is a customer concern that has become apparent while you are closing. It could be about their confidence in the product, its price or features, delivery dates, or something similar.

Objections need to be dealt with immediately and overcome in order to make the sale.

✚ An objection isn't necessarily a negative thing and can often be seen as a strong buying signal. A good salesperson can use an objection to close a deal using the SMS method.

Dealing with objections.

The SMS method is perfect for handling objections. You simply take the objection back over exactly the same steps I have just covered – Steps One, Two and Three.

When you are faced with an objection, listen attentively and acknowledge it. Then go back to Step One and ask one or more open-ended questions to explore the objection in order to fully understand it. Then go to Step Two and match it with a solution or explanation. Finally, confirm that the objection has been resolved with a closed-ended question.

Then it's back on and up the closing staircase.

For example, in the lawnmower store we have this scenario:

1 The salesperson has identified the customer's primary requirements through the use of open-ended questions.

2 The salesperson has matched those requirements with a specific machine in the store.

3 The salesperson has asked their first close:

Does this look like the sort of thing you're after?

Yes, replies the customer.

The salesperson moves up their closing staircase as the customer is looking fairly happy:

This machine is $550. Is this within your budget?

Look out, here comes the objection!

Not really, I love the machine but I was hoping to spend a bit less than this.

4 Back to Step One (open-ended question):

OK, what is your budget?

Or:

How far off your budget are we?

I was hoping to get something for around $500.

5 The salesperson assesses whether they are in range to close on a negotiated price or whether they should start looking at a less expensive machine that won't compromise the customer's requirements too much.

In this particular scenario, there happens to be a bit of fat in the price and the salesperson can meet the customer on what he is hoping to pay.

6 This objection has now become an opportunity to shoot right to the top of the closing staircase and close the deal:

If I was to sweeten the price a bit to bring it in line with your budget, would you agree to buy this machine?

Bingo!

Yes, I would. I like the machine, and if you can do it for $500, I'll buy it.

Done!

7 The salesperson writes up the order, affirms the sale and gets some value from the discount by asking if it would be possible to contact the buyer in the future for some feedback – the intention here may be to obtain a reference or testimonial.

——

An alternate scenario.

Of course, a salesperson won't always be able to bring the price down to meet the customer's budget. In this case, they are back on the closing staircase and have just hit the same price objection. The salesperson is over the customer's budget by $50, but this time there's no excess in the price to play with and it can't be reduced. However, the salesperson does have an understanding of the customer's requirements.

Here, the salesperson must return to the open-ended questions of Step One:

I have some other machines that have similar features and they might fit your budget. What sort of figure did you have in mind?

$500 is my limit, says the customer.

The salesperson then shows the customer a couple of machines that still (or almost) meet all his requirements, but definitely include his 'hot buttons'. After demonstrating both of them (Step Two), the salesperson returns to the closing staircase:

Both these machines fit your budget and requirements quite well – is there one that you prefer?

Yes, I think I prefer this one, says the customer.

The salesperson has successfully cleared this objection and is back at the closing staircase where they left off. They are now in a position to close the deal.

Good, this is a great machine and, in my opinion, it's the better of the two for your requirements. Are there any other issues?

(Nice close).

No, I'm happy with this, says the customer.

Great. Would you like me to make out an invoice?

Yes, please.

Done!

Alternatively, the lawnmower salesperson may have been able to do what the shaver salesman could have done; they could have continued to close with the FABs of the machine and then asked whether the customer could stretch his budget. You never know, if he likes the machine that much he may well find the extra $50.

————

The above examples demonstrate how pivotal closes are to selling.

Salespeople are often great at developing an understanding of what's required, but fail to make the sale due to their lack of closing skills.

Remember, if you use closed-ended questions to determine whether or not you have met the customer's requirements, you will be able to finalise the sale quickly.

Again, the great thing about the SMS method is that if you uncover an objection on the closing staircase, you know exactly what to do with it.

Return to Step One, acknowledge and explore the objection, then resolve it and get back on the closing staircase.

Alternatively, use the objection to close the deal; as in 'commit to buying and you will solve the objection'. This works no matter what the objection, as long as you can match it.

Bear in mind that an objection could be a concern regarding price or confidence in the product, or the customer may have seen another product they preferred elsewhere.

Whatever it is, don't see it as a problem.

View it as a chance to either explore the customer's requirements further or as an opportunity to close – on the condition that you solve the objection.

✚ Closing is so important. Not only is it where you finalise the sale, but also where you sort out the tyre-kickers from the genuine buyers.

You need to spend more time influencing the right people to buy and less time on those who will never buy. The closing staircase will quickly help you to determine if a prospect is genuine.

Using the objection to close the deal.

The following case study is a good example of how you can move between closes and open-ended questions to sort out objections with the SMS method.

A few years ago I was the sales director for a boutique multimedia production agency that specialised in top-end e-commerce solutions including web development, corporate video and a variety of digital corporate communication and presentation tools.

One of my sales team had been pitching to the country's leading telecommunications company for an intranet solution. It was a competitive pitch and although our presentation was strong, we were still a little unclear on the client's needs and seemed to be struggling to put the proposal together. The situation was a bit too messy for my liking but as the details were highly technical, I trusted that the team knew what they were doing and left them to it.

The salesman working on this project was called John and his desk was within earshot of mine. His phone rang one day and all I heard John say was: *Hmm ... hmm ... yes, oh I am sorry to hear that ... well that's a shame ... never mind, thanks for letting me know though, maybe next time, goodbye.*

He then looked up at me and declared that the telco's intranet job had fallen through. I asked him why and he explained that a competitor had won the job at a cheaper price. I asked him who the competitor was and how much lower their offer was but he didn't know. I was amazed and this motivated me to show him how he could have handled the situation better. I asked him if he would mind if I called the customer, and this is how the ensuing conversation went:

Hi Sarah, Julian here, John just told me that we failed to pick up the intranet job – is that correct?

Yes, she replied.

Sarah, do you mind if I ask you a couple of questions? It won't take long, I just want to check a couple of things.

Sure, but please make it quick, I'm very busy.

In my own mind, I established that we were on a new closing staircase and that we had just hit the objection, which was that they had a better offer from someone else. I went straight to Step One.

My first open-ended question was:

Why did we lose the job and was there anything we could have done to win it?

Sarah was very clear:

Look, we really liked your presentation and we would have preferred to work with your team. I loved your designs and your credentials were better than the others', but your proposal was too complicated and hard to understand. It also included things that we didn't really need and it was much more expensive.

I asked another open-ended question:

What was the competitor's quote?

$80 000, Sarah replied.

This was $40 000 less than our quote.

I asked her a couple of open-ended questions about the things we had offered that they *didn't* need and then tried some closes.

Sarah, we are very disappointed to have lost this job, especially as you preferred our designs. I know John really put a lot of work into this. If we were to get a new proposal to you within 24 hours – one which was comparable in price and functionality – would you reconsider?

To my surprise, she said: *Yes.*

My method was proving very robust. Look at what happened here, it's quite simple.

I had identified that we were in the closing stage of the sale and that we had uncovered an objection. So I took the negotiation back to Step One and asked some open-ended

questions to fully understand the objection. We were now re-matching the requirement and, if we did that well, we would be in a position to take the deal onto the closing staircase.

I ran downstairs with John to tell the producer what had happened and asked him if he could write a new proposal, which he was more than happy to do. I also asked him to call the client to get the specifications spot-on. Why not? We were still matching the requirements (Step Two). Sarah was fine with that and gave the producer the information he needed to write up the new proposal. We emailed it to Sarah that night (they were in another state) and I rang her the next morning and got straight back onto the closing staircase.

Did you get the proposal, Sarah?

Yes.

Have you had a chance to read it?

Yes.

Do you like it?

Yes – and I understand it.

Do you like it more than the competitor's?

Yes.

Nice closing staircase! Now it's time to close the deal:

Sarah, we are very keen to work on this project with you. Would you like to go ahead with us?

Yes, thank you, Julian.

Now for the affirmation:

Thank you, Sarah, I know you are really going to enjoy working with our team – they are very good and the design aspect of the job will be really cutting edge. You know that don't you?

I'm sure they'll do a good job.

Sarah obviously got what she wanted!

We won the deal back simply by uncovering the objection, asking the right open-ended questions, meeting the requirements and then closing with a series of closes. In fact, it was easy.

It is OK to break the rules of the SMS method now and then – to ask the occasional closed-ended question up front and the odd open-ended question when closing – but only if really necessary, otherwise the sequence of the method holds strong and true.

It's like putting one foot in front of the other – if you don't do it properly, you might trip.

What sort of closed-ended questions would work well for your product or service, keeping in mind your customers and your environment?

What sort of objections do you typically face? How can you creatively turn them into opportunities?

Step 4:

Affirming the sale.

Asking closed-ended questions.

Matching the need.

Asking open-ended questions.

The affirmation.

Affirming the sale is simply the act of responding to the customer's decision to purchase with strong positive and supportive statements.

If you have properly applied the SMS method to a transaction, you will be aware of your customer's original requirements and 'hot buttons'.

They have been convinced that your product or service meets their requirements and have just purchased it. The best thing you can possibly do now is thank them and show them how happy you are that you satisfied their original requirements.

This should happen once the sale has been closed and completed. The customer has signed or confirmed they are buying and are about to, or have already, made payment.

The best way to affirm the sale is to confirm that the customer has made a good, qualified decision by referring them back to the requirements that were discussed up front in Steps One and Two.

For example:

You are going to love wearing those shoes – you were looking for something to go with that outfit and they are perfect!

This outfit really complements your figure – you look fantastic in it. Well done and thank you, I am really happy for you.

Your keys, Sir, and may I say that this is the perfect car for you. You said you needed economy and space for your golf clubs, well, this one has the lot. Well done and thank you, you're really going to enjoy this model – it drives like a dream.

See, it's easy, but how many salespeople do it?

––––

Affirming the sale does three key things:

1 It deals with 'buyer's remorse' by making the customer feel confident in their decision.

2 It sets a positive tone for the customer to buy from you again (and refer others to you).

3 It eliminates stress for both you and your customer.

Beyond these three important points, affirming the sale is simply polite and should always be delivered with your gratitude.

1 Buyer's remorse.

How many times have you arrived home and unpacked your precious purchases only to start questioning your sanity as you realise that everything looks different in the bedroom mirror compared with how it did in the store and that you have also blown your budget!

Cold feet is a common customer experience after any purchase, whether large or small. All sorts of feelings come up and, more often than not, anxiety and remorse set in. For example:

Oh no! I've spent far too much!

My boss is going to question this decision – have I done the right thing?

Do these shoes look right? Oh, no! I'm not sure about them at all now!

Does my bum look big in this dress?

Worse still, some people listen to their doubting inner voice and come rushing back to return the item.

It happens all the time.

Affirming the sale is a simple and easy step that goes a long way towards dealing with buyer's remorse, thereby reducing the number of returns.

For example, how many savvy saleswomen understand the power of this statement:

Wow, that dress really suits your figure! Go on, turn around. Oh yes, it complements your shape perfectly!

2   A positive customer experience.

Affirming the sale leaves you and your customer with the sense that your last interaction was a very positive experience.

That's hugely important for anyone in business as it makes it easier for that customer to buy from you again.

Seventy per cent of sales across all business sectors are sales made to existing customers. Big business knows this and injects huge resources into customer loyalty programs – it's what most businesses are built on.

Basically, you want the customer to keep coming back and refer you to others. I don't think there is anything more satisfying than having a customer return to you again and again. To have them recommend you to others is priceless.

Affirmation really does help to build relationships, loyalty and trust.

✚ I love the idea that someone might say: *Hey, you should give Julian a call about that, here's his number. He really looked after me!* It's not just good for the ego, its great for the bottom line.

3 Dealing with stress.

Unfortunately, affirming the sale is a weak area for a lot of salespeople. They will often close the deal awkwardly and nervously, sometimes in a pushy way and usually without any understanding of the customer's original requirements.

They find it a fairly stressful part of the transaction so, once the customer has paid them, they can't wait to see them leave so that they can relax.

As mentioned earlier, stress levels can really rise in salespeople, and even lead to burnout.

Using the SMS method from beginning to end, including an affirmation of the sale, really helps to alleviate stress for both the salesperson and the customer.

———

More than an add-on.

Affirming the sale is an important part of any deal. It's more than just a nicety tacked onto the end of the transaction.

It brings a sense of professionalism and confidence into everything that you are trying to achieve. More importantly, it lends credibility to you and your business and should play a part in every negotiation.

Remember – the affirmation will be the last interaction that you have with your customer and is freshest in their memory. Make it a good one.

What positive affirmations can you offer with your particular product or service?

Conclusion.

Putting the 4 steps together.

Four steps to success.

The four steps that make up the SMS method follow a natural progression. In combination, they function as a complete sales cycle.

I would always recommend that you follow the steps in order. Start with open-ended questions, follow them by matching the requirements, close to confirm that the requirements have been met and then, after the final close, affirm the decision to buy. This logical sequence forms the complete cycle.

However, you may sometimes find that you have a number of smaller cycles running within your overall sales cycle, especially on longer or more complex negotiations. The SMS method is designed to accommodate that, *without* you having to reorganise its original structure. In other words, you can run four-step cycles within the overall four-step framework.

For example, you may need to make an appointment with a prospect – a deal which, in itself, could use the method's complete cycle. Although a complete four-step cycle is used to make the appointment, on the overall sales cycle you are just at the first step and still positioning yourself to understand the customer's requirements.

Once at the appointment, you might complete another sales cycle in order to position yourself for the next step. This could be to get higher up the executive chain of command and establish a meeting with more senior people, or to set up a demonstration or trial run. In addition, you might hit an objection while closing and this will prompt you to loop back around the cycle again to clear it.

The point here is that, on some occasions, you may need to be flexible and confident enough to propel one or more inner sales cycles within the overall sales cycle in order to move the transaction forward.

In these situations, you would simply follow the same four steps as outlined in the method, while keeping them within the overall four steps.

Once you are confident with the SMS method you will find it easy to track inner sales cycles. You may even have two of them running at once. Imagine trying to sell real estate to a couple who differed on their own requirements. That could be very challenging and may need to be tackled with two different approaches, but still within the four-step method.

Using inner sales cycles.

I have an excellent example of how a sales cycle can operate within the overall sales cycle. It's a rather long story but worth exploring because it illustrates inner cycles perfectly. In this particular situation I was involved in a very long sales cycle full of twists and turns that were out of my control but, in sticking to the method, I stayed on track to pull it all together. In fact, I honestly don't think I would have been successful in this case without the SMS method.

While I was working for the new media company, I had a telemarketer who made my appointments for me. We often talked about the SMS method and he used it regularly.

One day he excitedly told me that he had managed to secure an appointment to present – at a very senior level – to the country's biggest transport and logistics firm. Securing the appointment at such a high level was essentially a complete sales cycle while, at the same time, we were still very much at Step One of our overall sales cycle – establishing the firm's requirements through open-ended questions.

The following week I went out and presented. My presentation was going well until the prospect (whose name was Andrew) said suddenly:

Julian, I really like what you are showing me and we are most definitely in the market for this sort of thing, but I have to stop you here.

Sorry, Andrew, what am I missing? I asked (keeping to open-ended questions).

I have to stop you here, Julian, because I have a contract from DigitalXStream sitting on my desk which I have committed to sign today. It's similar to what you have shown me today, but I've agreed on something else with them. I am sorry.

DigitalXStream was one of our biggest competitors; it did look like we were a bit late on this one. Andrew would have travelled some way with them to get it to the contract-signing stage – both parties would have already done a lot of work. It wasn't looking good for us.

As I was packing up my laptop, I was about to suggest that Andrew look at us next time when my persistence suddenly kicked in. I do have trouble taking no for an answer sometimes and I decided to give my method another try.

As I considered my strategy, my objective changed and I decided to start a new sales cycle with the sole intention of stalling the contract signing. I knew that if I could, I might be able to buy enough time to position us to compete. After all, they had obviously approved a big budget already and Andrew had some very real requirements that I knew we could meet.

I also knew that our software was superior to DigitalXStream's in some way as our programmers were always talking about it, however not being particularly technical I wasn't sure what our point of difference really was.

I realised that as I had hit this objection, I just needed to start a new cycle with one open-ended question and see where things went from there.

So without really knowing where I was going with this, I politely asked:

Andrew, what is it about DigitalXStream's offering that you like?

His answer was quite interesting. He again referred to their product's similarity to ours but he was struggling to explain how it was better.

I sensed that he wasn't entirely convinced that DigitalXStream would deliver. Naturally, my next question was:

*What is it about DigitalXStream's offer that you **don't** like?*

Andrew didn't seem to mind my questions. He explained that he thought the DigitalXStream offer was OK but rather vague technically. After scratching the surface a little, I could see that he really did have some doubts about DigitalXStream.

By following the SMS steps within this inner cycle, I had established that Andrew's requirements (Step One) were not being fully met by DigitalXStream (Step Two).

I was now in a better position to try and stall the DigitalXStream deal by moving the conversation onto a closing staircase.

The first close on the closing staircase of my inner sales cycle was:

Andrew, is what I have shown you of interest?

Yes, he replied. *But as I said, Julian, I am committed to sign the DigitalXStream contract today!*

The second close on my closing staircase was:

Hypothetically, if the DigitalXStream deal wasn't there, would you be interested in continuing to discuss things with me based on what I've shown you?

*Yes, most definitely, but it **is** there,* he insisted.

I had moved the conversation onto a closing staircase and had got Andrew to acknowledge that if the DigitalXStream deal didn't exist we would be in a position to negotiate. However, I still hadn't done enough to stall the DigitalXStream deal. I needed another close but didn't have much to work with. As I tried to think of another question, a wild idea came to me. So with nothing to lose, I blurted out:

There are three basic questions you need to ask DigitalXStream before you sign that contract, Andrew. I know they can't deliver what I am showing you.

Andrew looked a bit sceptical, but I was on a roll now and could feel my confidence returning.

In fact, I continued, *you'd be wise to clear up a few things with DigitalXStream before you sign anything.*

Now that I had his attention, I reiterated my third close and clincher:

There are three questions you need to ask them, Andrew, because I'm sure they can't deliver what we can.

I knew if he bought this I could stall the DigitalXStream deal.

Would you like me to tell you what those three questions are, Andrew? (This is a close.)

Yes, Julian, if there's something I should know, I'd like you to tell me what it is.

Of course, I had absolutely no idea what those questions could be. I knew from previous conversations with our software programmers that DigitalXStream had issues but, for the life of me, I couldn't remember what they were. If only I had one of our programmers in the room with me! I was really winging it now but I'd clearly managed to sow some doubt in Andrew's mind – it was obvious that he already had some concerns.

I was slowly gaining enough traction to stall the DigitalXStream deal by closing on the three questions, even without knowing what they were. I had come so far, but all I could think of was:

The questions I have in mind are fairly technical, Andrew. To be fair to DigitalXStream and completely clear with you, they need to be worded exactly.

So my fourth close was:

Would you like me to write them out precisely in an email for you when I get back to the office? It would be best if one of our programmers helped me with the technical jargon. Then you'll be in a good position to ask DigitalXStream some qualified questions before you sign.

OK, Andrew agreed. *That sounds like a good idea ... in fact, I would appreciate that, Julian.*

This was the close I was looking for. My work here was done and I knew exactly what I had to do next. True to the SMS method, it was now time for a quick affirmation of this closed inner sales cycle:

Andrew, you won't be sorry – even if you go with DigitalXStream you'll be glad you've clarified everything. They'll respect your technical questions and think more carefully about being clearer with you in the future, and that has to be a good thing. I could tell that he was a cautious sort so I quickly added: *Better safe than sorry.*

To which he replied, *Thank you, Julian.*

Perfect! My method had come through for me yet again.

I knew that the director of programming would have the right questions for me back at the office, and she did. I asked her to write them out and email them to me. I then put an email together and sent it to Andrew.

I called him the next day. After some preliminaries, I asked him an open-ended question:

How did you go with DigitalXStream, Andrew?

I was now back on Step One of my original, overall sales cycle having completed the inner sales cycle to stall the DigitalXStream deal.

Well, they didn't like those questions, Julian. In fact, they got very angry and asked me why I was questioning them at this late stage. They were really annoyed and blamed me for not asking them earlier – we had a bit of a falling out over it, to be honest.

So, what's happening? What are you going to do? (Another perfectly natural, open-ended question.)

I don't know. I'm glad we're not moving forward with DigitalXStream, but it's back to square one for me. I need to get this presentation made and I'm running out of time.

My open-ended questions had done their job and the client's needs were now clearly established. I knew exactly where to go next.

Andrew, the presentation I showed you demonstrates that we have done plenty of work like this before. I am confident we could produce an amazing presentation for you. (I left it there to see how he responded.)

Julian, the stuff you showed me was really high quality. I'd be happy to talk further with you.

It was time to start closing the next step:

That's great to hear, Andrew – we would love to pitch for this job. Would you like me to set up a meeting with one of our producers so we can develop some ideas with you?

Yes, he replied.

Andrew was clearly pleased he hadn't gone ahead with DigitalXStream and I felt confident about having closed another small sales cycle.

My method was proving very faithful and it now required a quick affirmation:

That's great, Andrew. I know you've done the right thing here and I know that our team will be able to prepare a first-class proposal for you in no time.

Thank you, Julian.

Andrew seemed genuinely grateful; my hunch had paid off.

DigitalXStream obviously couldn't deliver what they had promised and were probably going to use this client's money to develop a solution they didn't already have.

We had the solution and were now in the perfect position to close the deal.

———

We had used three mini inner sales cycles to reach this point and we now had a live piece of business on the line. Although we were still at Step One of our overall sales cycle, we felt confident because we knew where we stood.

It was now time to further establish the client's requirements.

Andrew, to make things easy for you and so that you don't have to double up on work you have already done, it is probably best if you send us the brief you established with DigitalXStream. We can then prepare to meet with you and develop a proper brief with a full understanding of your overall objectives. What do you think?

This was a good open-ended question which, to my surprise, uncovered yet another requirement and gave the transaction a new direction.

That would be fine, Julian, but I think the best way forward is for you to meet with our advertising agency as soon as possible. They understand our requirements better than anyone and I would like to see what they think of your service.

No problem, Andrew. Can you give me the contact details of the person I need to speak to? I'll get straight onto it.

I was thrilled. I now knew enough about this job to realise it was worth hundreds of thousands of dollars.

Two weeks later, laptop in hand and full of confidence, I went to meet the contact at the advertising agency. Up until this stage of my career, I hadn't dealt with big creative agencies before. I was meeting with the CEO so I was a little nervous but I arrived on time and, after checking in with reception, was ushered into the CEO's office.

Peter will be with you in a minute, said the receptionist as she slipped out.

Fifteen minutes later, Peter entered the room. He curtly asked me to explain myself and 'get on with it'.

To say the introduction was cold would be an understatement; I was confused to say the least. After all, Andrew had given me the introduction and he was without doubt this agency's biggest client. We made small talk but it was just about how fit Peter was – that he ran every day and how important that was to him. It was like I was at the wrong meeting and after my big wins with Andrew I was now feeling pretty deflated.

I gave my presentation as best I could with Peter showing such a lack of interest. I kept asking myself what could possibly be wrong; this was definitely the coldest response my presentation had ever received. It just wasn't working.

After about twenty minutes I wound up the presentation and, with as much enthusiasm as I could muster, asked:

What do you think?

It's all right I suppose, I've seen plenty of this kind of thing before.

I was devastated – no one had ever said that to me before.

Our company show reel was cutting edge and it usually impressed the most disinterested audience. By now I was wishing Andrew had warned me about Peter, and I thought I might actually be in the wrong place.

I fumbled my way through some more open-ended questions but nothing seemed to be working. Peter's patience was running out and it was starting to show, along with my growing embarrassment.

He kept referring to DigitalXStream and asking me what was different about what I was showing him. He wouldn't buy into any of the explanations that I gave Andrew, and without getting into an argument I had little room to move.

Something was definitely wrong and the tension was becoming unbearable. I was now sweating, anxious and confused. Was Peter trying to humiliate me or was I way out of my depth? I just didn't know how to handle the situation.

Finally, like a cat toying with a mouse, Peter looked up at me and, as though stating the obvious, said:

You know I was pitching with DigitalXStream, don't you?

I'm sorry, I don't understand, I stuttered.

DigitalXStream and I were in partnership on this deal, and you, Julian, wrecked it just as the client was about to sign.

Peter was clearly very annoyed with me.

I was now petrified – my embarrassment had turned to fear. My cockiness about poaching Andrew's brief away from DigitalXStream drained away as quickly as the blood from my face. I was sitting in front of one of the major partners of a deal that I had totally sabotaged.

I was well aware of how much work must have gone into their proposal and pitch. I just wanted to get out of there as fast as possible – I was in the enemy's den. What would Peter do now? I have never been very comfortable with confrontation but there was nothing else for it – I needed to step up to the challenge.

I am really sorry, Peter, I had no idea you were involved with DigitalXStream.

It slowly dawned on me that Andrew didn't know his agency was financially involved with DigitalXStream, which seemed to me somewhat unethical. Surely the agency should have disclosed their interest.

What happened next was almost surreal. Although I was totally out of my depth and confronted by a highly charged and very disgruntled man, I also knew I had nothing to lose so I tried this:

Peter, you could always partner with us on our pitch. What do you think about that?

As the words came flying out of my mouth I was flabbergasted by my own stupidity, but I couldn't reel them back in. Here I was, throwing totally glib open-ended questions around the office of someone whose deal of the year I had just destroyed.

My anxiety deepened as I now expected this super-fit high-flyer to jump over his desk and thump me. I have never wanted to escape a place so desperately. I just wished that I had kept my mouth shut, especially as it now seemed my method had well and truly abandoned me.

Peter's response was breathtaking. It was as though he had been waiting for the conversation to get here but was equally surprised by how quickly it had arrived.

Well, that's not such a bad idea, Julian. Are you open to that?

The penny finally dropped. He didn't care that DigitalXStream's pitch had collapsed; he just wanted to be involved with the winning pitch. Peter was very direct and I knew from previous experience with such people that etiquette and politeness mean nothing to them while getting the best possible deal means everything.

I could hardly believe what had just happened, but I quietly gathered my faculties and persevered with my new inner sales cycle. I was quite relaxed now (more from relief than anything else) and went with this open-ended question:

Well, Peter, how do you think a partnership like this might look? What would you want out of it?

Then he really opened up.

I don't want a lot. I just want to be included as a consultant for the client. I will bill them directly and don't need to be included in your negotiations. I just want to be kept in the loop on your brief so that I can do the advisory work.

That was it? That's all he wanted all along?

Through the simple use of open-ended questions, Peter's requirements were gradually revealed.

That sounds fine to me, Peter, I replied.

Although I was much more relaxed and comfortable now, my next thought was that I should close the deal quickly and get out of there.

I just need to check this out with my team back at the office – is that OK with you? I asked.

Sure, Peter confirmed.

But he wasn't going to let me go that easily ...

Julian, you need my help to win this pitch – you will have trouble doing it without me.

I understood this veiled threat – he had a better relationship with the client than I did and Andrew wanted me to present to the agency before we moved forward. It was a no-brainer: work with the agency or he would kill our deal. I could live with that. I had plenty to think about on the long drive back to the office.

Upon arrival I told my team what had happened and asked them to cooperate and work with the agency. Everyone agreed it was a good idea. I then went back to meet with Andrew. I was in a perfect position to match his needs as I now had everything organised. It would be easy to close the deal from here. Peter had contacted Andrew and told him he thought we could deliver.

I assured Andrew that we could do the job with a series of closes:

Andrew, will you be happy working alongside the agency with us to get this project right?

Yes, Julian. They understand our product very well; I think that would be perfect.

If I bring the budget into line with the one that DigitalXStream pitched, would you be happy with that?

Yes. Do you think you could do that, Julian?

Oh I think so, Andrew, I continued confidently.

I realised that this would be the biggest deal I had sold so far in my time with the company.

Is there anything else you need me to go over with you, Andrew?

No, Julian, I think we'd better get a move on. I've lost a bit of time on this one.

Good. Would you like me to prepare an in-depth proposal?

Thanks, Julian. That sounds great.

I was now well into my final closing staircase. Once the proposal was presented, I simply closed around that with the following:

Are you happy with our terms and conditions?
Is this proposal consistent with your expectations?

In this way, we closed the deal.

My affirmation was easy as my company had asked me to hand the whole thing over to our executive producer.

Andrew, I am really pleased you have decided to work with us. I know we will be able to exceed your expectations.

I am also really happy that our executive producer is going to handle this job personally – you couldn't be in better hands. I'll call you from time to time but, really, you won't need me from now on.

Andrew was pleased with that and I could now move on to other things and wait for the commission cheque.

––––

This case study clearly illustrates how the four-step SMS method enabled me to guide this complex sale to a conclusion.

Although I used inner sales cycles along the way, I never deviated from the core method. I know that if I hadn't used it I never would have managed to stall the DigitalXStream deal but, more importantly, the method bailed me out when my back was against the wall.

Although this example was for a deal worth over a quarter of a million dollars, the same principles apply to all negotiations, whether large or small.

Combine the art and the science of sales.

This book presents a technique that is expressly designed to help you sell whatever it is you have to sell.

It is a simple, robust and effective method, much like a sketch or a map that allows you – the artist – to bring your personality, passion and values to the fore.

Artists are always conscious of two things: their own creativity and their audience. As a general rule, the most creative people are incredibly honest in their expression. This same rule applies to sales in that if you truly believe in what you are selling and present it honestly, you can gain incredible satisfaction from your work.

The SMS method allows you to be totally transparent with your customer, who will soon learn to trust you. It will give you the confidence to express your enthusiasm for your product or service which will, in turn, further influence your customer and help them to make the right decision.

Relationships are very important in sales and this book's four-step method is geared to help you build them. Remember, there is no point in building relationships if you aren't getting results, so try to let the warmer side of your personality shine as you build your negotiation.

If you apply the SMS method to your sales endeavours in a flexible and 'natural' manner, it will keep you on track to directly secure the deal while allowing you to remain relaxed and comfortable throughout – you may even start to have some fun!

I encourage you to practise negotiating and selling with the SMS method in mind. You will soon find that it is the perfect sales tool for every situation.

Happy selling!!

Notes.

www.ingramcontent.com/pod-product-compliance
Lightning Source LLC
Chambersburg PA
CBHW021600210326
41599CB00010B/532